PLANTING THOUGHTS
WITH WISDOM, WHIMSY & WONDER

PLANTING THOUGHTS
WITH WISDOM, WHIMSY & WONDER

Written, Compiled, and Illustrated by

KATHRYN GORDON CAMPBELL

ISBN: 1542729416
ISBN 13: 9781542729413
Library of Congress Control Number: 2017902949
CreateSpace Independent Publishing Platform
North Charleston, South Carolina

CONTENTS

PREFACE

How is your "thought compass" navigating your life?

Where are your "thought waves" carrying you?

What can you do to chart a better course?

We are usually told to address our actions and behaviors, yet becoming aware of what is going on inside is a better place to start. How we think is one step in our journey toward happiness and wholeness that many of us are not controlling as well as we could. Our desires are for fulfillment, but our thoughts are often navigating us in the opposite direction. Becoming aware of our thinking habits helps us to recognize how we might be sabotaging our happiness and contentment.

Some of us are more visual learners, and the illustrations in *Planting Thoughts with Wisdom, Whimsy & Wonder* help to set you back on the right course to a happy life. Begin your journey by taking twenty-one days to review thought-provoking and whimsical illustrations along with reading the deep, insightful quotes.

Inspired to *think* better *thoughts* by Philippians 4:8 in the Bible, I was surprised to discover that the acronym PREPLANT helped me better memorize this verse. This suggested to me that we must learn to think in a way that uplifts and learn to PREPLANT our minds to cultivate better thought patterns.

Philippians 4:8 says to think on whatever is

Pure **R**ight **E**xcellent **P**raiseworthy **L**ovely **A**dmirable **N**oble **T**rue

INTRODUCTION

This book is a compilation of wisdom quotes from outstanding books I have read and authors and teachers that I have heard over the past decade. As you take this step into more insight, my suggestion for reading this book's wisdom is to choose parts to review. The illustrations and related quotes are deep and thought provoking. You might read the opening pages and then simply look at all the illustrations. Open *Planting Thoughts with Wisdom, Whimsy & Wonder* on another day, and read one to three quotes per page. You may consider making a twenty-one-day commitment to review one illustration and read related quotes, each day advancing through this little wisdom book.

May you be blessed with more hope, happiness, and contentment!

~Kathryn Campbell

PREPLANT

Fill Your Thoughts and Think and Meditate on

Pure
Right
Excellent
Praiseworthy
Lovely
Admirable
Noble
True

**Think on whatever is true, noble, right, pure, lovely,
admirable, excellent, or praiseworthy,
and God will be with you.**

~Philippians 4:8, NIV

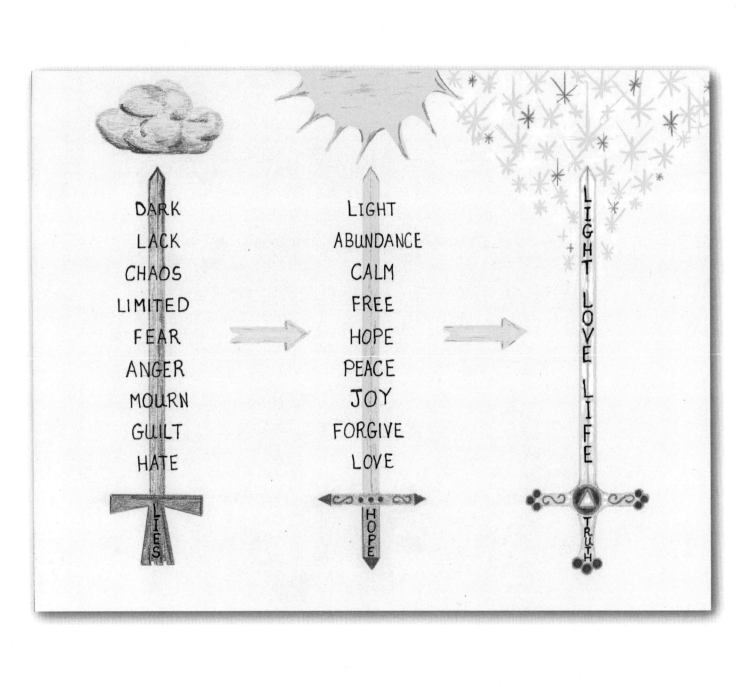

DOUBLE-EDGED SWORD

Our *free will* is like a double-edged sword. We either *bring to life that which benefits* well-being or blocks well-being by our thought patterns. ~Inspiration from Fernando in *Into the Wind*

But like a sword with two edges, your word can create the most beautiful dream, or your word can destroy everything around you. ~*The Four Agreements*, p. 26

The truth is the most important part of being impeccable with your word. On one side of the sword are the lies… and on the other side of the sword is the truth…Only the truth will set us free. ~*The Four Agreements*, p. 37

It is possible to change what we believe…but first we need to free our faith. And there is only one way to free our faith, and that way is through truth. The truth is our sword, and it's the only weapon we have against the lies. Nothing but the truth can free the faith that is trapped in the structure of our lies. ~*The Voice of Knowledge*, p. 127

Take the helmet of salvation and the sword of the Spirit, which is the word of God. ~Ephesians 6:16, NIV

Wherefore, may God grant His Grace unto you all that ye too may likewise succeed in your undertakings. For any man may be king in that life in which he is placed if so be he may draw forth the sword of success from out of the iron of circumstance. ~*The Story of King Arthur and His Knights*, p. 32

Creative power—God within us—is experienced as a double-edged sword: if received with grace, it blesses us; if received without grace, it drives us insane…"Miracles are everyone's right," says *A Course in Miracles*, "but purification is necessary first." ~*A Return to Love*, pp. 76–77

Positive & Negative Thoughts

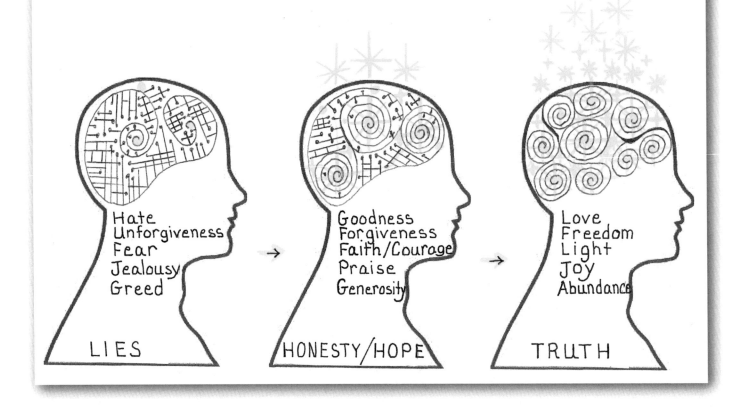

Hate
Unforgiveness
Fear
Jealousy
Greed

LIES

Goodness
Forgiveness
Faith/Courage
Praise
Generosity

HONESTY/HOPE

Love
Freedom
Light
Joy
Abundance

TRUTH

Your mind essentially serves you in two ways. It is a storage vault for information and past experience, and is also a transmitter for wisdom and common sense. ~*You Can Be Happy No Matter What*, p. 5

New answers don't come from what you already know in the computer part of your brain. They come from a change of heart, from seeing life differently, from the unknown, quieter part of yourself. ~*You Can Be Happy No Matter What*, p. 6

There is a mighty battle going on for control of your mind. Heaven and earth intersect in your mind; the tugs of both spheres influence your thinking…[God] created you with the capacity to experience foretastes of heaven. ~*Jesus Calling*, p. 274

You may have to develop new habits. If you've been negative for a long time, you should retrain your thinking from "I can't" to "I can." From "It won't happen" to "It will happen." Reprogram your computer. Load in some new software…When you believe…God's power is released! ~*Break Out!*, p. 127

A new idea, once accepted into our minds, becomes a *mental magnet*…Psychologists sometimes refer to this compilation of beliefs as our *mental maps*…Unfortunately, mental maps *always* contain errors…Correct and alter your mental map in ways that bring lasting and positive change. ~*The Four Doors*, pp. 15–16, 19

If most of the time you are thinking positively, you will turn on lights and be able to activate "greater portions of your brain. How can you turn on more of your lights?" In his book *Breakthrough!* Edgar Phillips tells us the answer is "Thoughts of a positive nature!"

The primary cause of unhappiness is never the situation but your thoughts about it. Be aware of the thoughts you are thinking. Separate them from the situation…There is the situation or the fact, and here are my thoughts about it. *~A New Earth*, p. 96

Be aware that what you think, to a large extent, creates the emotions that you feel. See the link between your thinking and your emotions. Rather than being your thoughts and emotions, be the awareness behind them. *~A New Earth*, p. 96

God has lit your mind Himself, and keeps your mind lit. *~A Course in Miracles*, p. 148

Our Garden of Thoughts

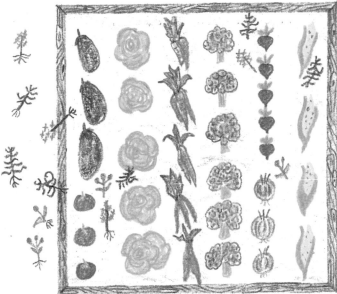

Pure
Right
Excellent
Praiseworthy
Lovely
Admirable
Noble
True

If our mind is like a garden and our thoughts are like seeds, what are we planting—fruits and flowers or weeds?
~Inspiration from Weldon, Wilson, Wordsworth, and Allen

Before we even begin to plant, we PREPLANT our garden by tilling, cultivating, and enriching the soil.

As you uproot, dig up, and toss out thought weeds, replace them with nourishing thoughts that fertilize the mind and encourage growth.

We reap what we sow in thought, word, and deed.

Every thought-seed sown or allowed to fall into the mind, and to take root there, produces its own, blossoming sooner or later into act, and bearing its own fruitage of opportunity and circumstance. Good thoughts bear good fruit, bad thoughts bad fruit. ~*As a Man Thinketh*, p. 11

Love and Laughter form the plough that prepares the ground for the seed. Remember this, if the ground is hard, seed will not grow there…Prepare the ground. ~*God Calling*, March 6

The fruit of the Spirit is love, joy, peace, patience, kindness, goodness, faithfulness, gentleness and self-control.
~Galatians 5:22–23, NIV

Pull out the negative thoughts and enrich them with positive thoughts; continue to cultivate this process so your growth flourishes.

We're all assigned a piece of the garden, a corner of the universe that is ours to transform. ~*A Return to Love*, p. 75

OUR THOUGHTS

Instead of Negative Thoughts	Move Toward	Positive Thoughts
Instead of Fear	Think	Love, Faith, Bravery, Courage
Instead of Guilt	Think	Forgiveness, Forgive Self, Learning, Peace
Instead of Doubt	Think	Hope, Love, Trust
Instead of Chaos	Think	Harmony, Order, Peace
Instead of Dark	Think	Light
Instead of Lack	Think	Abundance, Plenty, Gratitude
Instead of Judgment	Think	Curious, Forgive, Allow, Compassionate
Instead of Irritation	Think	Acceptance (of What Is), Calmness
Instead of Unforgiveness	Think	Forgiving, Grace, Freedom, Liberating
Instead of Boredom	Think	Contentment, Creativity, Awareness
Instead of Sadness	Think	Joyful, Love, Belief in Good
Instead of Evil	Think	Good
Instead of Disappointment	Think	Acceptance, Peacefulness, Gratitude
Instead of Confusion	Think	Harmony, Clarity, Tranquility, Serenity
Instead of Turbulence	Think	Calm
Instead of Sickness/Pain	Think	Health, Comfort, Vitality, Wellness

Instead of Negative Thoughts	Move Toward	Positive Thoughts
Instead of Stuck	Think	Flowing
Instead of Envy/Jealousy	Think	Praise, Contentment, Love
Instead of Resentful	Think	Goodwill, Gentleness, Forgiveness, Love
Instead of Problems	Think	Solutions, Answers
Instead of Ugly	Think	Beauty, Radiant, Spark
Instead of Regret	Think	Accept, Learn, Forgive Yourself
Instead of Discouraged	Think	Encouraged, Possibilities
Instead of Limited	Think	Limitless, Abundant
Instead of Stressed	Think	Relaxed, Release, Let Go
Instead of Cynical	Think	Skeptical, Goodness, Hope, Belief
Instead of Greedy	Think	Generous, Giving
Instead of Hate	Think	Love, Forgive, Believe in Goodness

Every negative and positive feeling is a direct result of thought... It's our thinking not our circumstances that determine how we feel... We forget moment to moment that we are in charge of our thinking.

~You Can Be Happy No Matter What, pp. 12, 14

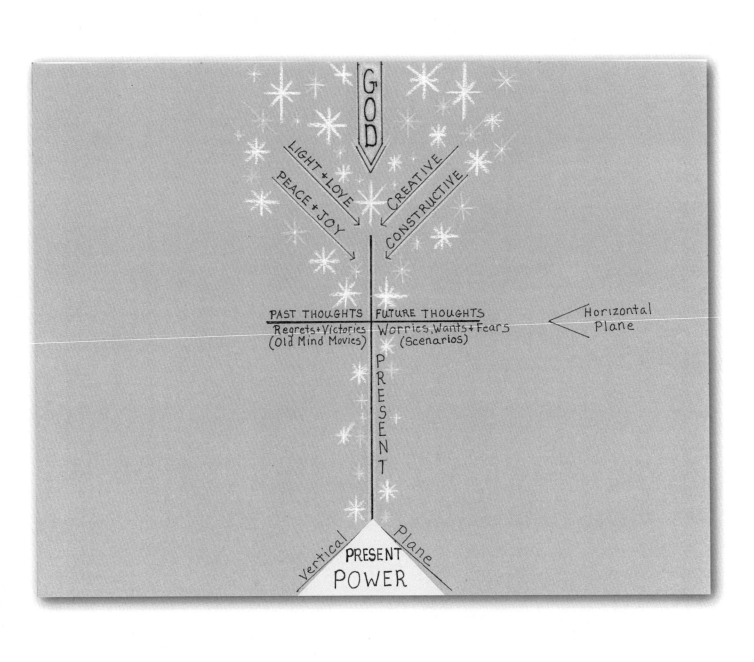

THE PRESENT

Most of us are living our lives on the horizontal plane. The vertical plane is where our *Now* power lies. ~Eckhart Tolle

Awareness is the power that is concealed within the present moment. This is why we also call it the present. ~*A New Earth*, p. 78

Do you spend more of your thought time in the present moment (the vertical plane) or in past and future thoughts (the horizontal plane)?

Our spiritual power lies in the present moment—the here and now.

Rather than rehash, ruminate on, and spiral in thought, release and return to the present moment, which opens the door to God's present power.

A renewed mind is presence focused. ~*Jesus Calling*, p. 35

Thankfulness heightens awareness of the present moment.

The present is always a chance to begin again, a light-filled moment. ~*A Return to Love*, p. 77

Yesterday's the past, tomorrow's the future, but today is a GIFT. That's why it's called the present. ~Bil Keane

HOPE

Hope's lamp lights your path.

Hope elevates your awareness.

Hope opens the way out of the maze of maize.

Hope spirals you up.

Hope strengthens you.

Hope is found in stillness.

Hope's path brings insight.

Hope is found through love.

Hope is a peaceful path.

Hope is like a golden cord connecting you to Heaven.
~*Jesus Calling*, p. 9

For I know the plans I have for you declares the Lord, plans to prosper you and not to harm you, plans to give you Hope and a future.
~Jeremiah 29:11, NIV

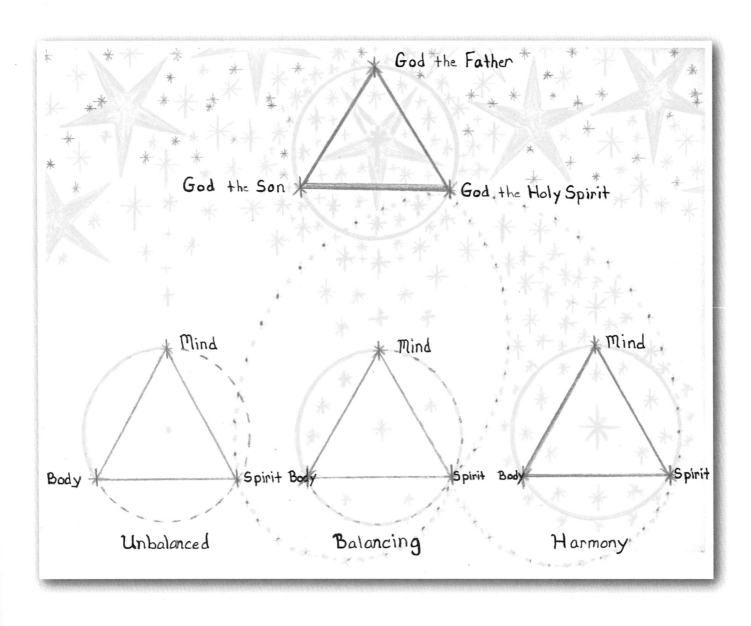

SPIRIT OF LIGHT AND LOVE

The kingdom of God is within you. ~Luke 17:21, NIV

God is within us, beside us, beneath us, above us and around us. ~Inspiration from Sister Angelica and from *Listening for the Heartbeat of God*

God gives the Spirit without limit. ~John 3:34, NIV

You have the Light, believe and trust in the Light...so that you may become sons of Light. ~John 12:36, AMP

You are a child of God...We are all meant to shine as children do. We were born to manifest the glory of God that is within us.
And as we let our own light shine, we unconsciously give other people permission to do the same. ~*A Return to Love*, pp. 190–191

Speak to Him thou for He hears, and Spirit with Spirit can meet- Closer is He than breathing, and nearer than hands and feet. ~Lord Alfred Tennyson

God is never hidden from us; we may be unintentionally hiding from him. ~Inspiration from the LDS sermon "Where Is the Pavilion?"

Always, from your very beginning, God's favor rests on you, and you are His beloved, shares Henri Nouwen in his book *Life of the Beloved*.

For God hath not given us the Spirit of fear; but of power, and of love, and of a sound mind. ~2 Timothy 1:7, NKJV

Thought Moments

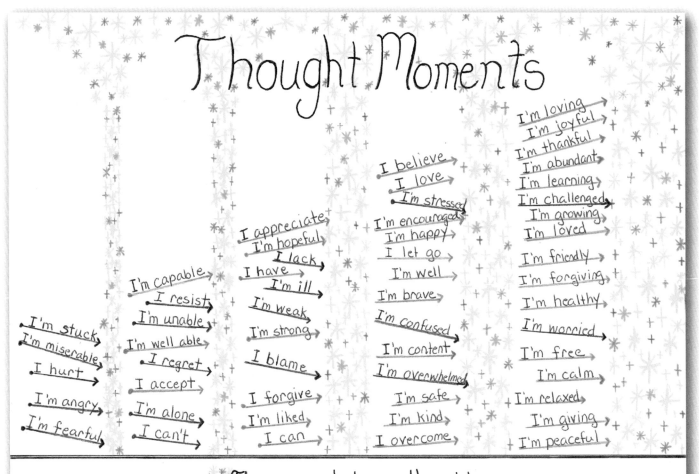

I'm stuck
I'm miserable
I hurt
I'm angry
I'm fearful

I'm capable
I resist
I'm unable
I'm well able
I regret
I accept
I'm alone
I can't

I appreciate
I'm hopeful
I lack
I have
I'm ill
I'm weak
I'm strong
I blame
I forgive
I'm liked
I can

I believe
I love
I'm stressed
I'm encouraged
I'm happy
I let go
I'm well
I'm brave
I'm confused
I'm content
I'm overwhelmed
I'm safe
I'm kind
I overcome

I'm loving
I'm joyful
I'm thankful
I'm abundant
I'm learning
I'm challenged
I'm growing
I'm loved
I'm friendly
I'm forgiving
I'm healthy
I'm worried
I'm free
I'm calm
I'm relaxed
I'm giving
I'm peaceful

The space between thoughts
God Presence
Present · Stillness · Focused · Serene · Peace · Joy · Life · Light · Love

Most of us have thousands of fleeting and not-so-fleeting thoughts every day, and positive thoughts have the power to lift us up.

We all talk to ourselves, sometimes out loud, but most of the time in the privacy of our minds…What are you in the habit of saying? *~You Are What You Think*, p. 42

Cleanse our minds of negative thoughts. *~The Alchemist*, p. 46

As we elevate ourselves by lifting up our thoughts, we will find it easier to lengthen the space between thoughts, opening ourselves more fully to the present moment.

The present is the space between thoughts. Our minds often become so busy that they forget to take a break.

One who is in the present moment is at one with what he or she does.

Stillness in thought is freeing. Stillness in thought brings reprieve and light. Stillness in thought turns the light bulb on.

This break from thoughts brings us into the present moment, the now, the gap, the present, stillness, serenity, awareness, alertness, harmony, tranquility, and the power and loving presence of God.

The key…Change your thoughts—your self-talk—and you change your life! ~*You Are What You Think*, p. 42

Choose ascending thoughts over descending thoughts, so our thoughts elevate.

[The Lord said,] Be still and know that I am God. ~Psalm 46:10, NIV

Usually, we first think we should stop doing and sit quietly. However, we might also consider this verse on *stillness* to mean that we should surrender our thinking to God and simply be present in the moment, relax our mind, be in the now, and let go of our thoughts. If we are working, we should be present in that experience.

Live fully in the present. ~*Jesus Calling*, p. 297

Light, Life, Joy and Peace flow freely through this gift [of Presence]. ~*Jesus Calling*, p. 39

THOUGHT COMPASS

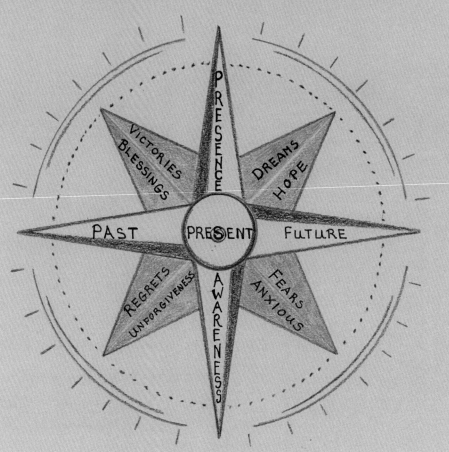

Past ~ Present ~ Future

Where is your compass leading you?

Move toward elevated thoughts and presence.

When you refuse to forgive, you hold on to the past, and it is impossible for you to be in the present...
Forgiving is a gift to yourself. It frees you from
the past, past experiences, and past relationships.
It allows you to live in present time.
When you forgive yourself and forgive others,
you are indeed free.
~Heart Thoughts, p. 91

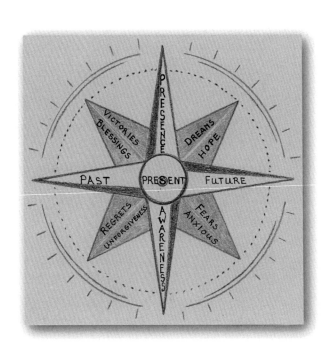

Anxiousness is a quivering and wavering of fearful thoughts.
When we are having anxious thoughts, we are not fully in the
present moment.

Awareness is our observation behind our thoughts. Being aware of our thoughts opens us up to loving insight
and a new perspective.

The secret is here in the present.
If you pay attention to the present, you can improve upon it.
And, if you improve on the present, what comes later will also be better…Live each day…confident that God
loves his children.
~The Alchemist, p. 103

Love
Belief
Light
Joy
Happiness
Love
Peaceful
Calm
Free
We Reap What We Sow
Generous
Abundance
Goodness
Appreciation
Forgiveness
Thankful
Hope
Worry
Regret
Unforgiveness
Fear
Envy
Hate
Anger
Guilt

THOUGHT WAVES

Our habits of thinking can raise or lower our thought waves or even keep us swirling.

Eliminating fearful thinking with thoughts of a higher nature diminishes the negative thought waves and expands our thought waves with belief, light, and love.

Words, no matter whether they are vocalized and made into sounds or remain unspoken as thoughts, can cast an almost hypnotic spell upon you. You easily lose yourself in them. *~A New Earth*, p. 25

The way we think is far more powerful than we often realize. *~Power Thoughts*, p. 5

When we believe lies, our minds can actually limit us. *~Power Thoughts*, p. 41

Our thoughts lead us, charting the course for our lives and pointing us in certain directions that ultimately determine our destinations in life. *~Power Thoughts*, p. 3

Drifting upward is always available, and movement is possible at any moment.

There are wonderful things in your life right now. Practice noticing them. When you turn your thoughts to the abundance you already have, you dissolve lack and draw more good things to you. Remind yourself daily of your blessings! ~Bob Wilson

THE WELLSPRING OF LIFE

The Holy Spirit opens to emanate from within each of us and is our ever-available wellspring.

Guard your heart, for it is the wellspring of life. ~Proverbs 4:23, NIV

Guard your thoughts, for they affect your wellspring of life.

Consider the heart to be the center of your being. Bring goodness, truth, beauty, understanding, peace, wisdom, joy, and love into your heart to keep it the wellspring of life.

Happiness is like a spring of living water.

Be silent and still to connect to the place within—where *happiness springs*! When we *connect with* the *Source* of Love, we learn that it is no longer necessary to earn and strive for happiness because it is already a part of who we are, shared Deepak Chopra in *Oprah & Deepak Expanding Your Happiness 21-Day Meditation*.

For the mouth speaks out of that which fills the heart. ~Matthew 12:34, AMP

"He who believes in Me...From his innermost being will flow rivers of living water." [By] this He spoke of the Spirit. ~John 7:38–39, NASB

Our true self guides us to the wellspring of lasting joy. ~Oprah Winfrey, (See *21-Day Meditation*)

Flow

Churning

Turbulent Thoughts

Free & Flowing

Current of Murky Misery

Currents of Calm & Contentment

You can change your conditions by changing your thoughts. ~*A Return to Love*, p. 140

The ego prefers that we not go into crisis. The ego prefers that a mild river of misery run through the background of our lives, never bad enough to make us question whether our own choices are creating the pain. ~*A Return to Love*, p. 150

Rest in My Presence brings Peace. God will help you…Peace like a quiet, flowing river cleanses, sweeps all irritants away. ~*God Calling*, January 5

When our minds become peacefully present and as our thoughts, feelings, and emotions harmonize, we can more joyfully and contently flow with the currents of life. ~Inspiration from *Einstein & the Art of Mindful Cycling*

This turbulent time will pass.

We tend to limit God's limitless goodness, so let God's infinite goodness flow into your thoughts.

Breathe in love and flow with life. ~*Heart Thoughts*, p. 79

My *streams of living water flow* through you. ~*Jesus Calling*, p. 318

Move out of the confusing current of misery by replacing negative thoughts with uplifting thoughts and free and flowing presence.

"Good will cannot flow toward you unless it flows from you." ~*Positive Thinking Every Day*, October 13

Missing the Mark

Light & Love

Truth · True · Joy · Peace · Gracious · Gentleness · Giving · Goodness · Gratitude · Forgiving · Generous

Lies · Hate · Fear · Unforgiving

God has given us the Holy Spirit to gently guide us to truth.

The Holy Spirit is our guide back to the bull's-eye, and the result is a loving change in our perceptions.

Sin is a word that has been greatly misunderstood and misinterpreted. Literally translated from the ancient Greek in which the New Testament was written, to sin means to miss the mark, as an archer who misses the target, so to sin means to "miss the point" of human existence. It means to live unskillfully, blindly, and thus to suffer and cause suffering. ~*A New Earth*, p. 9

When we choose not to follow the virtues of love, truth, and forgiveness, we miss the mark in experiencing our happiest selves—our true selves.

Our intellect is limited by design and wounded by sin. If we depend on our intellect to give us a full grasp of reality, we will miss the mark. ~*God Wants You Happy*, p. 100

Fear is using your Faith in reverse. ~Joel Osteen

Move from fear back to love and light.

The word "sin" means loveless perception…It means "you missed the mark." ~*A Return to Love*, p. 37

The Holy Spirit seeks out our innocence…where we tend to deviate from love are not our faults but our wounds. God doesn't want to punish us, but to heal us. ~*A Return to Love*, p. 93

FROM JUDGMENT TO TRUTH

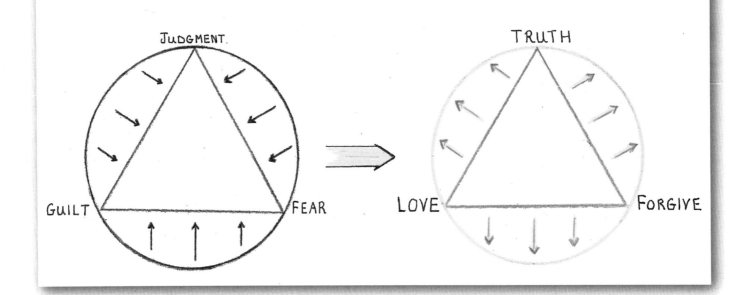

When guilt and fear team up with judgment, you are at the mercy of an unholy trinity that causes you to believe "There is something wrong with me." ~*Loveability*, p. 175

The basic fear of every ego is "I am not loveable." When you feel unloveable, you attack yourself with judgments like "I'm not good enough." ~*Loveability*, p. 177

The truth is you are loved. The truth is you are forgiven.

When we constantly judge ourselves, we contract and feel less than our true selves.

Fear puts us in bondage and causes us to fight, flee, or freeze.

Judgment can cause us to unmercifully attack ourselves and beat ourselves up.

Learn to love your mistakes as lessons learned, and gain a new perspective.

The less we judge ourselves, the less we judge others.

Without anxiety the mind is wholly kind. ~*Gifts from a Course in Miracles*, p. 64

Forgiveness does not mean approval. Jesus said, "Father, forgive them; for they know not what they do." ~Luke 23:34, KJV

Forgiveness undoes the blocks to love…Forgiveness is a return to love. ~Loveability, p. 174

Forgiveness frees us to love.

Believe that you are loved and loving, and extend that love.

OPEN HEART

Keep your heart wide open to God's whispers. Like an automatic camera lens...our heart is usually partially closed as a type of self-protective mechanism, or it opens and shuts quickly so that only a little light gets in. ~*God Wants You Happy*, p. 8

Your task is not to seek for love, but merely to seek and find all of the barriers within yourself that you have built against it. ~*Gifts from a Course in Miracles*, p. 92

Love waits on welcome, not on time. Gratitude goes hand and hand with love...The love of God...is everywhere. ~*Gifts from a Course in Miracles*, pp. 92–93

Be gentle with yourself and others as it is often fearful thinking that causes us to close our hearts.

Trigger topics can cause us, out of fear and the need to protect ourselves, to close the shutters to our hearts.

Whether we love, or close our hearts to love, is a mental choice we make, every moment of every day. ~*A Return to Love*, p. 19

For as he thinks in his heart, so is he. ~Proverbs 23:7, NKJV

The more we sow love upon everyone we meet, the better we prepare them for encountering God's personal, intimate, and unfailing love for them. ~*God Wants You Happy*, p. 12

When we read scripture, there is no need for fear of too much light. All that light is good for us. ~*God Wants You Happy*, p. 8

A mostly open heart...will always be filled with rays of light and joy...illuminate your life with His truth. ~*God Wants You Happy*, p. 8

Spirit of Freedom

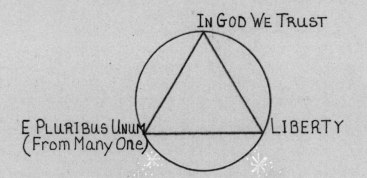

In God We Trust

E Pluribus Unum
(From Many One)   Liberty

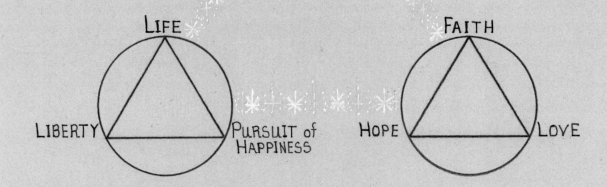

Life

Liberty   Pursuit of
                 Happiness

Faith

Hope   Love

A spirit of freedom gives us the opportunity to choose. As we liberate ourselves from negative thinking, we bring more love and light to those around us. As our thoughts and emotions heal, we have clarity of purpose and know how best to pursue our happiness and, in doing so, bring happiness to ourselves and others. When we comprehend from many one, we know that each one of us matters more than we realize. Give thanks that we have the freedom to choose how we think, how we speak, and how we act, which can ultimately bless us with a more joy-filled life.

Have FAITH in our Creator's goodness, love, and wisdom.

Have FAITH in yourself and your own abilities.

HOPE for a brighter tomorrow.

LOVE each other.

SHINING SPOKES

Rim of the World

GOD

We're like spokes on a wheel, all radiating out from the same center.

~A Return to Love, p. 31

⋏ ⋏ ⋏

Our Spirit-filled spokes shine bright.

⋏ ⋏ ⋏

As we connect to the love of God, we light up the world.

Life is...

"Before I formed you in the womb I knew you." ~Jeremiah 1:5, NIV

For you created my inmost being; you knit me together in my mother's womb. I praise you because I am fearfully and wonderfully made. ~Psalm 139:13–14, NIV

Surely you desire truth in the inner parts; you teach me wisdom in the inmost place, Cleanse me...wash me...Let me hear joy and gladness.
Create in me a pure heart, O God, and renew a steadfast spirit within me. ~Psalm 51:6–10, NIV

"[Jesus said,] 'I am never separated from you, nor from the presence of the Father, because I am a ray of his light, and I was sent to you to enlighten you. You are from...light.'" ~*Revelation of the Magi*, pp. 70–71

You and everyone on our planet have their "own pilot light" lit within. Although faint in some, the light "never goes out!" as Og Mandino shares in his book *The Greatest Miracle in the World.*

Believe in your destiny and the star from which it shines. Believe you have been sent from God as an arrow shot from His own bow. ~*The Four Doors*, p. 23

Thoughts Transform

A caterpillar can become a butterfly.

A grain of sand can become a pearl.

A lump of coal can become a diamond.

Are you not much more valuable?

~Matthew 6:26, NIV

Do not conform to the pattern of this world, but be transformed by the renewing of your mind.

~Romans 12:12, NIV

OPEN the DOOR

"So I say to you: Ask and it will be given to you; seek and you will find; knock and the door will be opened to you." ~Luke 11:9, NIV

Thankfulness opens the door to my [the Lord's] presence. Though I am always with you, I have gone to great measures to preserve your freedom of choice. I have placed a door between you and Me, and I have empowered you to open or close that door. There are many ways to open it, but a grateful attitude is one of the most effective…Learn the art of giving thanks in all circumstances. ~*Jesus Calling*, p. 215

"I have set before thee an open door and no man can shut it." ~Revelation 3:8, KJV

Think of the word love as a door. If you only look at the door, all you get is an idea about what love is; but if you are willing to move closer to the door, to open it, and to walk on through, you get to have an experience of what love is. ~*Loveability*, p. 10

Perhaps Love wants to show us more, and we are invited to open Love's windows and doors, as John Denver suggests to us in his song "Perhaps Love."

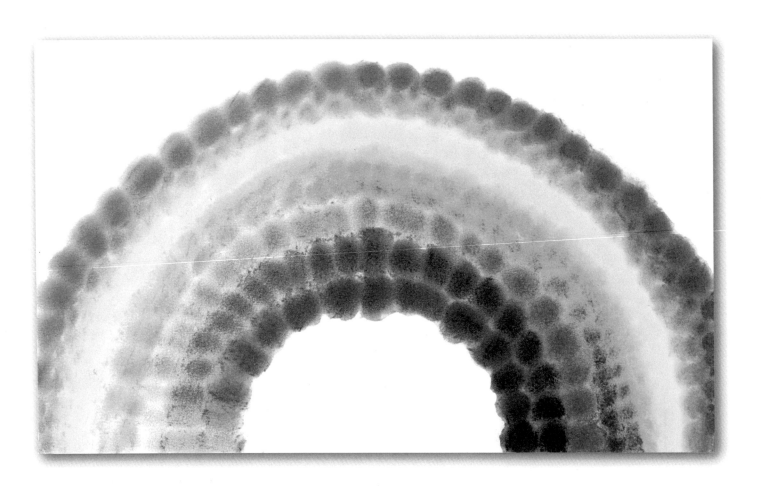

RAINBOWS REMIND

Rainbows remind me of WONDER.

Rainbows remind me of ABUNDANCE.

Rainbows remind me of BEAUTY.

Rainbows remind me of POSSIBILITIES.

Rainbows remind me to IMAGINE.

Rainbows remind me to BELIEVE.

Rainbows remind me to be THANKFUL.

Rainbows remind me we are LOVED.

Rainbows remind me to LOVE.

Heaven's Healthy Seasonings

For health, vitality, and aliveness, keep on affirming that the powerful life force of God is flowing through your mind, your spirit, your body. ~*Positive Thinking Every Day*, June 7

Sunshine helps to make glad the heart of man. It is the laughter of Nature. Live much outside. My medicines are sun and air, trust and faith. ~*God Calling*, August 17

Jesus said to his disciples: "Therefore I tell you, do not worry about your life...Life is more." ~Luke 12:22, NIV

Laugh more, laugh often. Love more. I am with you. I am your Lord. ~*God Calling*, March 11

"You are the salt of the earth...You are the light of the world." ~Matthew 5:13–14, NIV

Practice peace of mind and forgiveness.

Your thoughts and cultural beliefs affect your body. ~Dr. Christiane Northrup

Metabolism is the sum total of all the chemical reactions in the body, plus the sum total of all our thoughts, feelings, beliefs and experiences. ~*The Slow Down Diet*, p. 8

Ahhh...Breathe in fresh air. Walk, breathe, and meditate on love, joy, and peace.

Breathing freely releases the mind from the bondage of negative thoughts. *~Breathe Deep, Laugh Loudly*, p. 16

Harmony in spirit, mind, and body go hand in hand with health.

Savor life in the moment when time stands still. ~Dr. Christiane Northrup

Take "thyme" today to be thankful.

Breathe deep. Laugh loudly. Live well. ~Dr. Judith Kravitz

BEGIN ANEW

PREPLANT
your heart, mind, and soul for joy!

**Each day, we begin anew
with what we choose
to think and do.**

~**Bob Wilson,** www.balancedweightmanagement.com

**Release fearful thoughts.
Let go! Let God!**

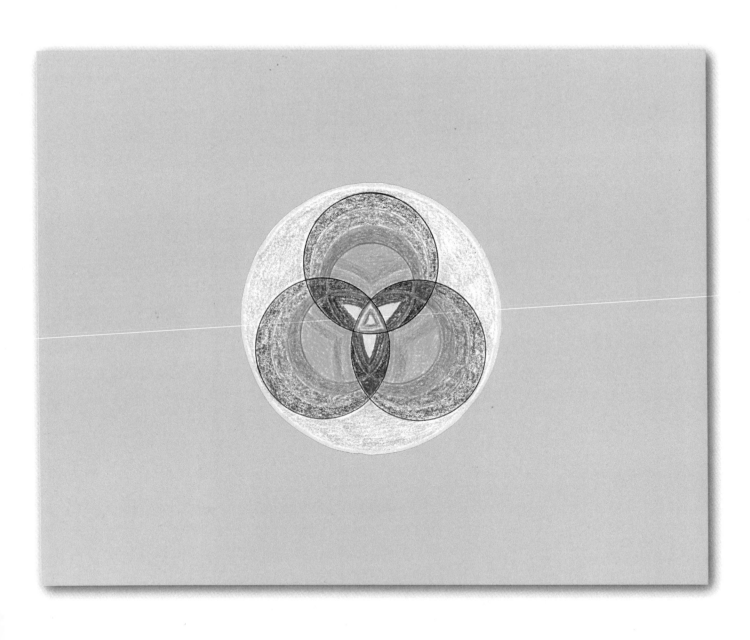

INSPIRATION

Inspired by This Bible Verse:

Finally...whatever is true, whatever is noble, whatever is right, whatever is pure, whatever is lovely, whatever is admirable—if anything is excellent or praise-worthy—think about such things.

~Philippians 4:8, NIV

ACKNOWLEDGMENTS

For permission to use copyrighted material, the author gratefully acknowledges the following:

Carlson, Richard.
From the book *You Can Be Happy No Matter What.* Copyright © 1992, Revised 1997 by Richard Carlson, PhD. Reprinted with permission of New World Library, Novato, CA. www.newworldlibrary.com

Coelho, Paulo.
Two brief quotes from p. 103 from *THE ALCHEMIST* by PAULO COELHO and TRANSLATED BY ALAN R. CLARKE. Copyright © 1988 by Paulo Coelho. English translation copyright © 1993 by Paulo Coelho and Alan R. Clarke. Reprinted by permission of HarperCollins Publishers.

David, Marc.
The Slow Down Diet by Marc David. Rochester, VT: published by Inner Traditions International and Bear & Company, ©2015. All rights reserved. http://www.Innertraditions.com Reprinted with permission of publisher.

Eckhart Tolle. Permission granted for use of quote by Permissions at Sounds True.

Evans, Richard P.
   Reprinted with permission of Simon & Schuster, Inc. from *THE FOUR DOORS: A Guide to Joy, Freedom, and a Meaningful Life* by Richard Paul Evans. Copyright © 2013 by Richard Paul Evans. All rights reserved.

Eyring, Henry B. "Where Is the Pavilion?" *BYUtv*. Sermon from the General Conference. Salt Lake City: The Church of Jesus Christ of Latter-Day Saints, 2012. Used by permission.

Hay, Louise. *Heart Thoughts*. Carlsbad, CA: Hay House, Inc., 2012.
   Used by permission of Hay House, Inc.

Holden, Robert. *Loveability*. Carlsbad, CA: Hay House, Inc., 2013. Used by permission of Hay House, Inc.

Joel Osteen. Quote from Lakewood Church Sermon /Joel Osteen Ministries.

Keane, Bil. *Family Circus* (Cartoon by Bil Keane; Ran August 31, 1994). Used by permission from Jeff Keane.

Kravitz, Judith. *Breathe Deep, Laugh Loudly: The Joy of Transformational Breathing*.
   Sandwich, NH: Free Breath Press, 2002. Used with permission. All rights reserved. Transformational Breath® is registered trademark of Breath Ventures, Inc. USA.

Landau, Brent.
   Brief quotes from pp. 70-1 from *REVELATION OF THE MAGI* by BRENT LANDAU. Copyright © 2010 by Brent Landau. Reprinted by permission of HarperCollins Publishers.

Oprah Winfrey from *Oprah & Deepak Expanding Your Happiness 21-Day Meditation*. Used by permission.

Osteen, Joel. *Break Out!* New York: FaithWords, 2013.

Meyer, Joyce. *Power Thoughts*. New York: FaithWords, 2010.

Morris, Jonathan.
Five brief quotes from pp. 8, 12, 100 from *GOD WANTS YOU HAPPY* by FATHER JONATHAN MORRIS. Copyright © 2011 by Jonathan Morris. Reprinted by permission of HarperCollins Publishers.

Northrup, Christiane MD. www.drnorthrup.com. Used by permission.

Peale, Norman Vincent.
Reprinted with the permission of Fireside, a division of Simon & Schuster, Inc. from *POSITIVE THINKING EVERY DAY: An Inspiration for Each Day of the Year* by Dr. Norman Vincent Peale. Copyright © 1993 by Dr. Norman Vincent Peale. All rights reserved.

Ruiz, don Miguel with Janet Mills.
From the book *The Voice of Knowledge* © 2004, Miguel Angel Ruiz, M.D. Reprinted by permission of Amber-Allen Publishing, Inc. San Rafael, CA www.amberallen.com All rights reserved.

Ruiz, Miguel.
From the book *The Four Agreements* © 1997, Miguel Angel Ruiz, M.D. Reprinted by permission of Amber-Allen Publishing, Inc. San Rafael, CA www.amberallen.com All rights reserved.

Russell, A. J.
From *God Calling* by A.J. Russell. Published by John Hunt Publishing Ltd, www.johnhuntpublishing.com. Used with permission.

Stoop, David.
DAVID STOOP author of *YOU ARE WHAT YOU THINK*. Grand Rapids, MI: Revell, a division of Baker Publishing Group. Copyright © 1982, 1996 by David Stoop. Used by permission.

Tolle, Eckhart.
   A New Earth. New York: Plume, a member of Penguin Group (USA) Inc. 2005.

Vaughan, Frances and Roger Walsh, eds.
   Gifts from a Course in Miracles. Edited by Frances Vaughan, Ph.D. and Roger Walsh, M.D., Ph.D. Copyright ©
   1983,1986,1988 by Foundation for Inner Peace. New York: Jeremy P. Tarcher/Putnam, 1995. Publisher: Used with
   permission from Frances Vaughan and Roger Walsh. Vaughan and Walsh (eds.).
   Foundation for Inner Peace https://www.acim.org/index.html
   Frances Vaughan http://www.francesvaughan.com/
   Roger Walsh www.drrogerwalsh.com

Williamson, Marianne.
   Brief quotes from pp. 19, 31,37, 75-7, 93, 140, 150, 191 from *A RETURN TO LOVE* by MARIANNE WILLIAMSON.
   Copyright © 1992 by Marianne Williamson. Reprinted by permission of HarperCollins Publishers.

Wilson, Bob. Copyright © 2001-2017 Bob Wilson BS, DTR. All Right Reserved. www.balancedweightmanage-
   ment.com. Used by permission.

Young, Sarah.
   Jesus Calling. Nashville, TN: Thomas Nelson, 2004. Used by permission of Thomas Nelson. www.thomas-
   nelson.com.

REFERENCES

A Course in Miracles (The Text; The Workbook; The Manual for Teachers).
Compilation © 2005 by New Christian Church of Full Endeavor, Ltd.
This 2007 edition published by Barnes & Noble, Inc. by arrangement with A Course in Miracles International.
New Christian Church of Full Endeavor.

Allen, James.
As a Man Thinketh. Brief quotes, including inspiration from page 11 quote, "A man's mind may be likened to a garden." New York: Barnes & Nobel, Inc. 2007. Originally published in 1902.

Angelica, Sister. Sister Angelica on EWTN (Global Catholic Network).

Chopra, Deepak, MD. *Oprah & Deepak Expanding Your Happiness 21-Day Meditation.*

Ducey, Jake.
Into the Wind. Inspiration from page 61 quote "Free will is a double-edged sword…" Cardiff, CA: Waterfront Publishing, 2013.

Irvine, Ben
Einstein & the Art of Mindful Cycling: Achieving Balance in the Modern World. New York: Metro Books, 2012.

Mandino, Og.
  The Greatest Miracle in the World. New York: Bantam, 1977.

Newell, J. Philip.
  Listening for the Heartbeat of God: A Celtic Spirituality. Mahwah, NJ: Paulist Press, 1997.

Nouwen, Henri J. M. *Life of the Beloved*. Crossroad Publishing Company, 1992.

Phillips, Edgar. *Breakthrough!* San Francisco: Business and Professional Books, Inc. 1981.

Pyle, Howard.
  The Story of King Arthur and His Knights. London: Anness Publishing Ltd. 1996.

Weldon, Mel. Inspiration from quote "My mind is a garden."

Wilson, Bob. Inspiration from quote "Our mind is the garden." Copyright © 2001-2017 Bob Wilson BS, DTR. www.balancedweightmanagement.com. All Rights Reserved.

Wordsworth, William. Inspiration from quote "Your mind is a garden."

AUTHOR BIOGRAPHY

Kathryn Gordon Campbell graduated from UCLA and worked in Los Angeles for seventeen years as a CPA and tax director. Upon moving to Carlsbad, California, Campbell transitioned into being a full-time homemaker, spending her time raising a family, and volunteering with various school, church, and community activities.

An avid traveler, Campbell has visited many places throughout the United States and such places as Europe, South America, and Southeast Asia. In line with her belief in positive thoughts and natural ways to wellness, she recently became a dōTERRA essential oils wellness advocate and consultant. Campbell has always loved books and has been a member of book clubs for close to two decades.

Campbell has been married to her husband—whom she met while attending UCLA—for thirty-six years. Together, they have three children.

Made in the USA
Lexington, KY
03 August 2018